The Life and Work of...

Georges Seurat

Paul Flux

Heinemann Library
Chicago, Illinois

Designed by Celia Floyd
Illustrations by Sam Thompson
Originated by Ambassador Litho Ltd
Printed and bound in China by South China Printing Company

06 05
10 9 8 7 6 5 4 3

Library of Congress Cataloging-in-Publication Data
Flux, Paul, 1952-
  Georges Seurat / Paul Flux.
      p. cm. -- (The life and work of ...)
Includes bibliographical references and index.
Summary: Through images and brief text, presents an overview of the life
and work of French painter Georges Seurat.
  ISBN 1-58810-603-9 (lib. bdg.)   ISBN 1-4034-0001-6 (pbk. bdg.)
  1. Seurat, Georges, 1859-1891--Juvenile literature. 2.
Painters--France--Biography--Juvenile literature. [1. Seurat, Georges,
1859-1891. 2. Painters.] I. Title. II. Series.
  ND553.S5 F58 2002
  759.4--dc21
                              2001003972

Acknowledgments
The author and publishers are grateful to the following for permission to reproduce copyright material:
p. 4, AKG Photos; p. 5, Courtauld Gallery, London; pp. 6, 22, 24, Roger Viollet; p. 7, Metropolitan Museum of Art, New York; p. 9, César de Hauke; p. 11, Private Collection; pp. 13, 23, Bequest of Stephen C. Clarke; p. 15, National Gallery, London; p. 16, Ben Fathers/AFP; p. 17, Bridgeman Art Library, Art Institute of Chicago; p. 18, Musée d'Orsay, Paris; p. 19, Tate Picture Library; p. 20, Magnum Photos; p. 21, Musée des Beaux-Arts, Tournai; pp. 25, 29, Musée d'Orsay, Paris; p. 27, Courtauld Institute Galleries.

Cover photograph reproduced with permission of National Gallery, London/Bridgeman Art Library.

Every effort has been made to contact copyright holders of any material reproduced in this book. Any omissions will be rectified in subsequent printings if notice is given to the publisher.

Special thanks to Katie Miller for her comments in the preparation of this book.

Some words are shown in bold, **like this.** You can find out what they mean by looking in the glossary.

Contents

Who Was Georges Seurat?

Georges Seurat was one of the finest French artists. He lived more than 100 years ago. People today still enjoy his pictures of the people and places he knew.

Georges invented a new way of painting, using tiny dots of color. The dots worked together to make the new, brighter colors he wanted in his pictures. This style is called **pointillism.**

The Bridge at Courbevoie, 1886

Early Years

Georges Seurat was born in Paris, France, on December 2, 1859. The family home was near the Parc des Buttes-Chaumont. He showed the park in some of his paintings.

This drawing of a woman sewing is Georges's mother. Georges was always interested in drawing people. This was one of the first pictures he ever made.

The Artist's Mother, 1882–83

Art School

When Georges was eighteen he went to art school. His teacher **encouraged** him to copy drawings by the **Old Masters**. This helped him learn to draw better.

Georges saw a painting by the German artist, Hans Holbein, in the Louvre Museum in Paris. This is the copy Georges made. It is very much like Holbein's painting.

Richard Southwell, after Holbein, about 1877

In the Army

In 1879, Georges was in the army for a year. He was sent to Brest, a small town on the French **coast.** He did many drawings of boats, beaches, and the ocean while he was there.

10

Man Leaning on a Parapet, 1881–83

Georges returned to Paris in 1880. He painted this picture of a person leaning on a bridge over the Seine River. People by the river became one of Georges's favorite **subjects.**

A Special Showing

In 1883, when he was 23, Georges had a painting shown at the **Salon**. This was a special **exhibition** in Paris where the best artists showed their work. This was a great honor for Georges.

This is the picture Georges had shown at the Salon. It is a drawing of his close friend Aman-Jean. This was the only painting Georges had at the Salon in his lifetime.

Portrait of Aman-Jean, 1883

Painting with Dots

In the spring of 1883, Georges began his first large painting. It showed people swimming. This was not chosen to be at the 1884 **Salon**. Rejected paintings were shown in their own **exhibition**. Georges' picture was hung in the cafeteria!

Bathers at Asnières, 1884

In *Bathers at Asnières*, Georges showed how color could be used in a new way. He painted with small dots. The dots mix together in the viewer's eye to make all the different colors of the painting.

The Modern Painter

In the winter of 1884 to 1885, Georges worked on another large painting. It was of an island in the Seine River, called La Grande Jatte. It was a very popular place for people to walk in the 1880s.

When the painting was shown, many people did not like it. They thought a picture of people walking by the river was not a good **subject** for a large painting.

Sunday Afternoon on the Island of La Grande Jatte, 1884–86

Growing Fame

After he painted *La Grande Jatte,* Georges became better known. Other artists began to copy his way of painting. This picture is by Paul Signac, one of Georges's close friends.

Women at the Well, 1892, by Paul Signac

Le Bec du Hoc, Grandcamp, 1885

In the summer of 1885, Georges stayed in the town of Grandcamp, Normandy. The town is on the **coast** of France. He wanted his paintings to show what the sea looked like there.

To Catch the Moment

Georges spent the next summer in the **coastal** town of Honfleur. He still wanted to paint pictures of light, water, and the seashore. Georges worked outside to get his colors as **accurate** as possible.

The Shore at Bas-Butin, Honfleur, 1886

This is one of the pictures Georges painted at Honfleur. Many other artists also began to paint with dots like Georges. This way of painting is known now as **pointillism**.

Mystery of the Circus

Some people said that Georges could only paint **landscapes.** So he looked for something to paint in which people were the focus. He chose the circus, which was a very popular show in Paris.

Invitation to the Sideshow, 1887–88

Georges often visited the Circus Corvi in Paris. People at the circus are usually happy. Georges chose not to show them having fun in this picture. He used dark colors to show sadness.

23

A Normal Life

In 1888 Georges spent his summer at Port-en-Bessin on the French **coast**. He did many drawings and **sketches** that he used later in his paintings. He seemed very happy.

Georges painted six pictures of Port-en-Bessin that summer. He liked the peace and stillness. He tried to show this in his paintings.

Port-en-Bessin: Outer Harbor at High Tide, 1888

Love and a Family

In 1889 Georges met and fell in love with Madeleine Knobloch. They lived together in Georges's art **studio**. In February 1890 they had a son, whom they called Pierre Georges.

Young Woman Powdering Herself, 1890

This is the only large **portrait** Georges ever painted. It shows Madeleine in front of a mirror. She is putting on her makeup.

Final Days

On March 29, 1891, Georges died suddenly of a disease called **meningitis.** He was only 31. His son died a short time later of the same disease.

This was the last painting Georges worked on. He had not finished it when he died. Georges is famous for paintings that made everyday people and things seem special.

The Circus,
1890–91

29

Timeline

1859	Georges Seurat is born in Paris on December 2.
1878	Georges joins the Paris School of Fine Art.
1879	He spends one year in the army.
1880	He returns to live in Paris.
1883	Georges has his first picture shown at the **Salon**. He begins to paint *Bathers at Asnières.*
1884	Georges helps start the Society of Independent Artists.
1886	He shows his paintings at the **Impressionist exhibition.** He finishes *Sunday Afternoon on the Island of La Grande Jatte.*
1887	He shows his paintings with the Belgian artists, "The Twenty."
1888	Georges spends the summer painting at Port-en-Bessin on the **coast**. He finishes *Invitation to the Sideshow.*
1889	He meets Madeleine Knobloch and lives with her at his **studio**.
1890	Georges and Madeleine have a son, Pierre Georges. Georges spends the summer painting at Gravelines, on the coast.
1891	Georges dies suddenly from **meningitis** in Paris on March 29.

Glossary

accurate as near true as possible

coast where the land meets the sea

encourage to persuade someone to do something

exhibition public display of works of art

Impressionists group of artists who showed the effect of light and movement in their pictures

landscape picture of the countryside

meningitis disease that affects the brain and causes headaches and high temperature

Old Masters great artists from Europe who lived a long time ago

pointillism way of painting using tiny dots of color

portrait painting of a person

Salon France's official art exhibition, which was held every year

sketch unfinished or rough drawing or painting

studio room or building where an artist works

subject something shown in a painting

Index

More Books to Read

Flux, Paul. *Color.* Chicago: Heinemann Library, 2001.

Flux, Paul. *Pattern and Texture.* Chicago: Heinemann Library, 2001.

Flux, Paul. *Perspective.* Chicago: Heinemann Library, 2001.

More Artwork to See

The Gardener. 1882–83. Metropolitan Museum of Art, New York, N.Y.

Landscape at Saint-Ouen. 1878 or 1879. Metropolitan Museum of Art, New York, N.Y.

The Lighthouse at Honfleur. 1886. National Gallery of Art, Washington, D.C.

1/4/16